GOD'S VISION, YOUR DECISION

JEROME STOKES

GOD'S VISION, YOUR DECISION

ISBN: 0-9740880-2-1

Published by

LIFEBRIDGE
B O O K S
P.O. BOX 49428
CHARLOTTE, NC 28277

Printed in the United States of America.

COVER DESIGN BY JR GRAPHICS

DEDICATION

*To my loving wife, Marsha, who is a true
example of a God-fearing woman and companion.
She has stood with me through all we have encountered.
Her input into the activities of our lives has been
major in our achievements.*

*To my parents, Robert and Lovella Stokes,
for their superb spiritual and parental guidance.*

*To the CRL family of believers for
their love and support.*

CONTENTS

INTRODUCTION

Each week in churches across America and around the world, believers gather to worship the Lord Jesus Christ. Parishioners enter their particular sanctuary and participate in the spiritual program that is offered.

Many Christians "go with the flow" and give little thought to what is actually happening. They simply attend church, sing a few hymns, give an offering, hear a sermon, greet other believers and then go home.

As you will discover on these pages, there is so much more to the Body of Christ than this.

God has a specific vision for His church – and the course He sets for a local assembly is based on that divine plan. You and I are directly involved. The way we relate to His heavenly purpose determines the extent to which we effectively walk in it – and fulfill it. The vision is God's and must not be ignored or pushed aside by His people.

After reading this book, I believe you will understand

that the Almighty has great benefits in store for those who discover and properly identify with what the Lord sees for His church. Once we grasp this concept, our lives in the Body of Christ will never be the same. We will begin to experience an increased flow of God's blessings. It swings wide the doors to abundance in both the spiritual and natural realms.

I am convinced that certain believers suffer in many areas of their lives because they have not connected with God's vision - and they will continue to experience a deficiency until they embrace it. The way we relate to the Father's plan determines the kind of life we will have here on earth and throughout eternity.

It is my prayer that this book will find it's way into the hands of church members everywhere. If these scriptural principles are followed, I believe they will produce unity and cause spiritual growth - both to the reader and the church.

– Dr. Jerome Stokes

~

CHAPTER ONE

GOD'S VISION FOR HIS CHURCH

If you have been active in a local church, you've no doubt heard the pastor say, "Let me share with you the vision I have for this ministry."

Yet, the average church member doesn't seem to relate to the words spoken. Often, they simply dismiss the phrase as the pastor's personal plan or desire – not understanding that what is being articulated is *much* more substantial.

When those who stand behind the pulpit walk sincerely with the Lord, they become communicators of *God's vision*, and are greatly used to help bring about its fulfillment.

A POWERFUL DECLARATION!

There's a verse in Proverbs that many can recite by heart, yet often they fail to understand it's significance:

Where there is no vision, the people perish:
but he that keepeth the law happy is he.

PROVERBS 29:18

What is this *vision* that, when missing, will cause people to become weak – and perhaps even die? The word itself is basically defined as "discernment" or "foresight." It is from the Greek word *chazown,* meaning "revelation."

The famous verse from Proverbs has often been misinterpreted because the word *vision* has taken on new meaning since the publication of the King James Bible in 1611. According to the proper translation, it literally means "prophetic vision."

By inserting those two words into the verse, it reads: *"Where there is no prophetic vision, the people perish."*

~

Prophetic vision is passed from heaven to earth and from God to man.

What a powerful declaration! No longer is this a reference to natural discernment or foresight. It denotes the revelation of what God has declared in heaven, and is now manifesting on earth.

It is prophetic because it has not been fully revealed. You see, God unveils portions of His plans and purposes as they are being carried out.

As we will discover, prophetic vision is passed from heaven to earth and from God to man. It is precious in the Father's sight, so the Lord discloses it in His own special way.

10

Please understand, there must be absolute sincerity on the part of all believers as they relate to (and become active in) fulfilling God's vision. When fully understood, the impact is both revelational and far reaching.

ONLY ONE VISION

Let me say at the outset that what God sees for the church *originated* with Him and was *determined* by Him. The Lord did not consult with anyone concerning what it should include or how it would be instituted. He is One and so is His vision.

There are hundreds of thousands of churches established throughout America and around the world, yet God has only *one* plan for His church. From the beginning, it has been His divine purpose that when any person walks into a place of worship that honors His Son, they would find His vision in operation. Though we are laboring in different parts of the vineyard we are still involved in carrying out the single plan mandated by God.

I am convinced that believers who worship in a true Christian church will find themselves practicing the same activities as Christ. When He came into this world, He was sent by the Father to be our perfect example (1 Peter 2:21) – not only in suffering but also in living. He is still our role model for completing the mission of the church:

- He preached (Matthew 4:17).
- He called disciples (Matthew 4:18,19).
- He taught (Matthew 4:23).

11

- He healed the sick (Matthew 4:24).
- He cast out devils (Mark. 5:1-20).
- He fed the hungry (Mark. 6:35-44).
- He sent disciples (Matthew. 10:1-28).
- He raised the dead (John 11:1-46).

Until the day Christ ascended to heaven, He demonstrated what it meant to carry out God's hopes and dreams for the church. As they walked with Him, the disciples became students in the fulfillment of the Father's purpose.

FAR-REACHING IMPACT

The oneness of God's vision is of great significance. As believers we should never make the mistake of thinking that our actions and deeds are *local* because we are involved in local church assemblies. Our participation in the church we attend extends far beyond the walls of that particular sanctuary – it stretches to the entire Body of Christ.

> *Our participation in the church we attend extends far beyond the walls of that particular sanctuary – it stretches to the entire Body of Christ.*

Our neighborhood church ministers to a specific group of people, yet the vision being accomplished is God's. That's why we must be fully aware that our actions in Baltimore or Phoenix affect the church in Bosnia or Paraguay. Let me be more specific:

- If we fight pastors at the local assembly, we are fighting pastors everywhere.
- If we are lazy in our home church, we are promoting slothfulness everywhere.
- If we tithe at the church we attend, we are tithing to His vision worldwide.
- If we labor at the local assembly, we are laboring in every place the Great Commission is being carried out.

Whatever we undertake, good or bad, we are in essence doing the same thing wherever God's vision is being fulfilled.

A UNIVERSAL RETURN

Are you beginning to see why all believers must be cognizant of how they conduct themselves in the congregation where they are a member? That behavior, whether respectable or regrettable, will bring not only a local return, but a *universal* harvest.

This is the reason that being in conflict against your church can result in harsh consequences. Speaking for myself, to avoid risking God's judgment, I would rather leave my church and go to another than to participate in squabbling and unrest.

Over the forty-five years of my walk with God, I have seen dozens of people become upset over particular issues in the church. Instead of prayerfully attempting to resolve the problem, or moving on, they remained where they were and continued in a highly disgruntled state. As a result, many became a detriment to the work of the Lord – not only in that church, but in the Body of Christ.

I cannot over-emphasize this point. There is no such thing as an attack against one local congregation. The missile may be launched toward a given church, yet the assault affects the entire work of the Lord. The same holds true for the positive spiritual activities we undertake. If we are diligently involved in God's work, our labor will benefit believers *everywhere*.

CONFLICT AND GLOOM

Today, the Father's vision for the church often seems distorted – out of focus. Never have I seen so much conflict among Christians. There are denominations pitted against denominations, churches against churches, pastors against pastors – and, sadly, even races against races.

How can God's ultimate purpose be properly advanced when these conditions prevail? The picture becomes even more dismal when we add the fact that within the Body of Christ there is a scarcity of instruction in Godly living.

Instead of sermons that constantly " pump up" believers, we need messages to remind us that the promises of the Holy Scriptures are *conditional* – they depend on righteous living. That is what will bring those who are born again into unity and keep us focused on God's great purpose. Only when we work together will we accomplish what the Lord intends for His church.

THE OPPOSITION

God's vision is being fulfilled, but not without opposition by Satan.

It should come as no surprise that the staunch enemy of God is also the arch enemy of His people. Since the day the church was established, Satan and his legion have fought to topple it. Why do these attacks against believers persist? It is because of our relationship with the Lord and the assign-

> *The staunch enemy of God is also the arch enemy of His people.*

ments we have been given. We are opposed by the enemy because we are being used by God to carry out His divine will.

Satan's attacks are not only to destroy us, but to unravel the plans of the Almighty. As we will examine in Chapter Five, much of his strategy is devoted to the destruction of pastors.

Here are just nine methods the enemy uses in his desire to hinder and foil God's vision:

1. He uses disobedience.

Failure to obey weakens believers and renders them ineffective in their roles and responsibilities.

15

2. *He uses ignorance.*
The lack of knowledge promotes error and failure –
and can bring destruction (Hosea.4:6).

3. *He uses a lack of understanding.*
This can cause us to adopt improper paths and codes
of conduct. As a result, life's decisions are greatly
obscured.

4. *He uses division.*
Satan focuses on causing corporate weakness by
breaking down fellowship. Since God uses us both
individually and collectively to advance His purpose, we must maintain unity. *"And if a kingdom be
divided against itself, that kingdom cannot stand"*
(Mark. 3:24).

5. *He uses envy.*
Jealousy drives a wedge in the spiritual atmosphere,
and encourages negative kingdom relationships. The
enemy causes us to envy the successes or the advan-
tages of others.

6. *He uses financial difficulty and lack of resources.*
Since the advancement of God's vision often requires finances, Satan will aim every arrow in his
arsenal to keep us impoverished.

7. *He uses pride.*
The enemy attempts to prevent believers from
humbling themselves to one another – and from
identifying with the vision some other Christian
may have.

8. He uses selfishness.

Satan strives to cause us to hold on to our resources, rather than distribute them.

9. He uses greed.

Excessive desire for the things of this world distorts our view of the Father's divine purpose.

~

These are only a few of the evil methods used by the enemy as he attempts to hinder God's plan. Yet, in spite of Satan's opposition, the vision of the Lord marches on. As the Word declares, the gates of hell cannot prevail against the Church of the Living God (Matthew 16:18).

CHAPTER TWO

~

DETERMINED, DELIVERED AND DISTRIBUTED

I trust you have come to the realization that I am not simply discussing vision in this book. I am talking about *The* Vision – God's desire for His church as it operates in an earthly setting of steadily declining spiritual and moral values. Only the Creator knows how to deal with such conditions. Only He understands fully what is occurring and how it can be effectively handled.

In this chapter we answer these important questions:

- Who determines the vision?
- How is it delivered?
- Who distributes the vision to the church?

1. THE VISION IS DETERMINED BY GOD

Every aspect of the church is the result of the foresight of God. He is Jehovah Elohim – the Lord Our Creator. The first verse of the Bible declares, *"In the beginning God created the heaven and the earth"* (Genesis 1:1). He brought everything into existence.

> *All things were made by him: and without him was not anything made that was made.*
>
> JOHN 1:3

As designer of the universe, He knows best how to deal with the people and elements of His creation. He also is the all-knowing Omniscient One who possesses full knowledge of everything that takes place in heaven and earth.

~

God is the only One qualified to develop and establish a plan for His people.

This means that God is the only One qualified to develop and establish a plan for His people. None other can effectively implement a blueprint in a manner that fulfills His divine will. Only *He* knows fully what His vision for the church is – and only *He* can utilize humanity in the achievement of it.

THE FATHER KNEW

Does God's divine view for His creation include man? Of course. We are His cherished children, made in His likeness and image. The fact that God formed man from the dust of the earth is proof that we are included in His plan. The Father is not "last minute" in His nature. That which He does, He knows *beforehand*.

Prior to the events recorded in Genesis:

- God knew that He would create man.
- He knew that Adam and Eve would fall and bring sin upon the human race.
- He knew that humanity would have to be reconciled unto Him.
- He knew that Jesus would come into the world to atone for the sins of man.
- He knew that through His plan of redemption the church would be established.
- He knew that He would institute the fivefold ministry (Apostles, Prophets, Evangelists, Pastors and Teachers) of the church (Ephesians 4:11).
- He knew that believers who comprise the Body of Christ would need pastors.
- He knew that He would have to choose those who would ultimately become spiritual leaders over His people.
- He knew that He would use pastors in His plan for making His vision become reality on the earth.

21

THE MISSION

God's design for His church reflects the nature of the activities of the Body of Christ. The Christian church is basically concerned with the matter of *relationships* – God's relationship to man, man's relationship to God, and man's relationship to man.

What is the primary focus of the church? *People.*

For that reason, we are charged to provide the opportunity and climate for God's love to be experienced and enjoyed by persons within its fellowship. Through this body of believers, we are to communicate the message of Christ. Jesus told His disciples to go into all parts of the world and teach all nations (Matthew 28:19).

In addition to world evangelism, the mission of the church includes:

- To love God (Matthew 22:37).
- To glorify the Father (Ephesians1:5-6; 2 Thessalonians 1:12).
- To manifest God's grace (Ephesians 2:8).
- To baptize believers (Acts 2:38).
- To teach those who have been saved (1 Timothy 4:6; 2 Timothy 2:2).
- To provide Christian fellowship (1 Corinthians 1:9; 2 Corinthians 8:4).
- To provide believer edification (1 Corinthians 14:26; Ephesians 4:11-12).
- To discipline believers (Romans 16:17).
- To bear one another's burdens (Galatians 6:2).

- To restrain and enlighten (2 Thessalonians 2:6-7; Matthew. 5:16).
- To promote all that is good (Galatians.6:10).

Each of these mission functions were determined by God. He established what the church would do based on His pre-ordained plan.

2. THE VISION IS DELIVERED TO PASTORS

Before I formed thee in the belly I knew thee; and before thou camest forth out of the womb I sanctified thee, and I ordained thee a prophet unto the nations.

JEREMIAH 1:5

The office of pastor is not a position that one simply chooses to occupy. It is far from the preparation of a secular career.

Those who shepherd God's flock are

The office of pastor is not a position that one simply chooses to occupy.

called by the Most High. *He* chooses the individuals that He ultimately appoints to become pastors.

During my ministry journey I have seen individuals

enter the pastorship for the following misguided reasons:

1. To make up for their apparent failure to achieve success in their natural careers.
2. To make a name for themselves.
3. To promote their own popularity.
4. To feed their ego through pastoral leadership.
5. To establish a means to acquire more money.
6. To achieve a position of power.

THE "CARRIERS"

As a minister of the Gospel, I have learned the vital importance of continually examining my motives. Failure in ministry comes like an onrushing train when the intentions of a pastor are misdirected.

> *Those who lead congregations must see themselves as "vision carriers" in the Body of Christ."*

Those who lead congregations must see themselves as "vision carriers" in the Body of Christ. God has called and equipped them to bring His divine purposes to the people.

An essential part of God's calling includes imparting what is in the heart of the Father. Remember that (1) God determines the vision and (2) He delivers it to pastors.

As those men and women of God become involved in

their heavenly assignments, the Lord will unveil more and more of what He expects.

THE PATH TO PROGRESS

I've heard ministers comment, ' "I don't know where God is taking me."

That is natural. There is only one vision, but God must reveal to pastors the way it is going to be carried out in each ministry setting. We know the Lord is leading us to a specific destination, yet we don't have the details of how He will take us there.

Vision, therefore, is *progressive* in its revelational nature. As various parts of the plan are completed, God will reveal subsequent portions. Before long we see a *real sense* of progress in ministry.

I say "real sense" because countless churches have a calendar overflowing with programs and activities, yet have missed the process of vision fulfillment. A ministry is simply spinning its wheels if it is not carrying out God's divine expectations.

Read these next words carefully. *Many speak about God's vision "for their ministries," but I believe we should view ourselves as one ministry in the process of fulfilling God's vision.*

Some pastors may be more gifted in certain areas than others, however, we must recognize our common mission. If there is one vision and various ministries carry out a portion of it, then surely we should have much in common. The originator of each component is God – and we are helping to bring our assigned portion to fruition.

IN HARMONY

Since God's purposes are Spirit-revealed, it is incumbent on pastors to lead Spirit-led lives. It is the only way they will be in one accord with what the Lord is doing.

Here is the Father's plan:

1. God knows the specifics of the portion of the vision assigned to each pastor.
2. As ministers are led by the Spirit, they will operate in accordance with the will of God.
3. As the Spirit reveals God's will, the pastor will engage in the activities of vision fulfillment.

To operate outside of the Spirit's leading is like trying to fly without wings. Lack of advancement is guaranteed. You not only fail God, but hinder the progression of everything He envisions.

The Spirit reveals, leads and empowers, however, the Father's plans will only be accomplished through us when the Spirit is *followed*. We are used by God, but only He brings the actual fulfillment.

Since the Lord is working through us, we must be worthy instruments for His use. That's why it is imperative that we live holy lives (1 Peter 1:16).

A DIVINE ORDER

More than once I have been asked, "Why is God's vision

delivered to pastors, rather than to lay members?"

I didn't write the Bible, or define the order of things. That was done by the Almighty – the same God who established how His church was to be organized (Ephesians 4:11). If the Lord chooses to ordain pastors to communicate His will, who am I to rearrange the divine plan?

I often hear lay members speak of what they can or cannot see in relation to the vision. One man said, "I believe I know what is best for this ministry."

Certainly, Godly counsel must be welcome in the House of the Lord, but never forget, God reveals His vision through pastors.

God reveals His vision through pastors. Any church member operating otherwise is out of order.

Any church member operating otherwise is out of order.

There have been several instances when men and women under my pastoral leadership felt that they knew, better than me, what direction the ministry should take.

Thankfully, my scripture-based response helped the people see God's plan. I reminded these individuals of my calling and relationship with the Lord. I further reiterated that the assigned vision for the church – spiritually, administratively and operationally – was being progressively revealed through me.

Whether a minister has been recently called to a church,

or is the founding spiritual leader, his place in the divine order of things is the same. The pastor has been appointed as a shepherd over the flock for a reason – to lead according to God's purpose.

BIRTHED IN MY SOUL

In my case, the Lord birthed the ministry of our congregation – The Church of the Redeemed of the Lord (CRL) – within me, and brought it forth through me.

From personal experience I can tell you that the vision given to a pastor is always accompanied by heavy burdens and demanding requirements.

We began the work in Baltimore in 1985 with six members. At the time I was working as a computer systems analyst.

I vividly remember the first building we looked at for our future church home. It was a storefront – and definitely not a facility to be desired.

I was beginning to see the structure not as it was, but through the eyes of faith.

As I was being interviewed by the person representing the owner, I was glancing around the delapidated building and was actually getting excited. Why? Because I was beginning to see the structure not as it was, but through the eyes of faith. I envisioned what it could become. God planted the seeds of something

28

great in my soul!

One week later, when I learned we had been approved to lease the building, I was highly elated.

REBUILDING THE WALLS

The task of remodeling was enormous. With some volunteers who caught the vision, we began changing the design of the storefront and spent countless hours remodeling, repairing and painting. Sometimes I had help, and other times it was just me. I felt like Nehemiah, rebuilding the walls of Jerusalem.

The days were long and arduous. When I took off my "computer analyst" jacket I put on my work clothes and started hammering. We worshiped in that facility for twenty-eight months.

Sundays were certainly no days of rest. Trading in my Peugeot, I purchased a church van for the ministry – and made two trips to pick up parishioners before conducting the morning service. Then it was two more trips before we could have lunch.

On Sunday evening I started the process over again. This was in addition to holding down a full-time job, plus my pastoral duties of preaching, teaching, counseling and visitation. To me, this was all for the glory of God.

I COULD "SEE" IT

When the second building was acquired, I experienced the same challenges as the original facility, but on a broader scale. Even though the church had grown significantly I was still a participant in every major renovation project. At times my workload seemed unbearable, yet I knew where God was leading. I could *see* it.

Even when the growth of the church allowed me to resign from my secular employment, the long hours never seemed to shorten. Physically drained, I was only able to continue by the energizing power of God.

Again, we entered into a lease agreement for a building where more work was required. I prayed, "Lord, you know I am going to need some help on this project."

Feeling the urgency, I painted that facility almost single-handed.

A point of crisis came when we founded the CRL Community Support Center. We purchased a building next to the church which had previously been a saloon. Once more, major renovation was the order of the day. It was the next verse of the same song – not enough volunteers to stay with the project – and not enough money to hire outside workers.

After we rebuilt the first floor, which had rotted out, many helpers faded into the woodwork. I appreciated what they could do, however, they had too many "personal matters" to attend to.

"Lord," I said, "if I have to do it alone, I will."

To say I was weary and burned out from ongoing ministry obligations is an understatement. The congregation had now grown to several hundred.

SHOULD I GIVE UP?

It was a Friday. I arrived at the new facility that

morning and surveyed the enormous amount of work that still needed to be done.

That day, I was the only person who reported for work. Suddenly, a deep pain and overwhelming weariness washed over me and I felt I wanted to give up. Sitting in the middle of the floor with tears flowing uncontrollably out of my eyes, I looked up to heaven and cried, "Please Lord, give me the strength to continue."

I labored alone all day in the building.

That evening, while I was teaching a Bible class I felt extremely weak and at times my mind was in a fog. Somehow, the Lord helped me make it through.

I found myself sitting in the middle of the floor with tears flowing uncontrollably out of my eyes.

After the session, I was bombarded with parishioners who wanted to share their problems. Politely, I cut the conversations short because of my physical and mental state.

Finally, I told my wife, Marsha, "I'll meet you at the house." We had each driven separate vehicles to church that evening.

THE EMERGENCY

I walked to my car and began the journey home. Almost immediately, I felt a strange sensation in my body – as if I were going through some unfamiliar changes. It was difficult for me to continue driving and I thought, "I'm just a couple of minutes away from a medical facility, I'd better head that direction."

I hurried to the hospital. This was unusual for me because I had never really been sick. The Lord had always blessed me with good health. On this occasion, though, I realized that I had not used wisdom and had literally worn myself out.

> "Don't worry. The doctors are going to check me out and I'll phone you in a few minutes."

When I arrived at the emergency room, they registered me and I immediately called my wife and told her were I was. "Don't worry. The doctors are going to check me out and I'll phone you in a few minutes."

She was extremely concerned and wanted to rush to my side, but it was late and I asked her to remain at home.

After my exam, a doctor told me, "Reverend, you are suffering from extreme exhaustion. My advice is that you should go home, get in bed and stay there at least two weeks."

I followed the first part of his advice. I drove myself home and rested all day Saturday. On Sunday, I couldn't help myself and preached both services – and shared with the church my emergency room diagnosis.

A WOUNDED SPIRIT

On Monday, disobeying the doctor's orders, I was back in the unfinished facility. I felt like I had entered solitary confinement. No one showed up to help with the work.

Surrounded by a building that desperately needed repair, my physical body slowly began to sink to the floor, and my spirit began to sink with it.

In vain, I attempted to pull myself together. My mind began playing tricks on me and it seemed the walls, windows, floors, and ceilings began to sing a song of my loneliness, while at the same time calling me to repair their flaws and make them ready for use. As the chorus sang, my already tired body felt more pain and hurt than I had ever experienced.

Prostrate on the floor of that old building, all I could do was weep from the depths of my soul. Every ounce of my body seemed wounded; there was no part of me left to provide encouragement.

Satan must have had a jubilee when I began to think the worst: "Members of the church don't love me. After all I have done, why isn't someone willing to help? Why would so many Christians allow a faithful pastor to experience such a degree of disappointment?"

The questions came nonstop – especially concerning the members of our church. "Do they love the Lord? Do they love the church? Do they understand God's vision for our future?"

My tears continued to flow until there seemed to be none left. Finally, the Lord lifted me from the depths of my depression and self-pity. I stood up in the middle of that building. "Lord," I said, "it makes no difference whether anyone comes to help or not, I know what You have told me. I will not stop until the work is completed."

WHAT I LEARNED

In February, 1995, we purchased a third piece of property with room to build a sanctuary to seat over two thousand. Even then, it was difficult for some of the members to catch the vision. Instead, we encountered those who had become comfortable with the present and were not ready to launch forward.

By this time, I had endured enough resistance to know that what the Lord promises He will perform – regardless of the trials along the trail. God raised up a workforce within the ministry.

Here's what I learned in the process. If we are faithful to the vision, the Lord will provide the needed resources. Two years later we moved into the new facility and continue to rejoice at what God has done.

If we are faithful to the vision, the Lord will provide the needed resources.

I have shared this experience not to edify myself, but to emphasize the fact that many pastors experience hardship, and even life-threatening situations in the process of following the Master's mandate. Why do they continue? It is because of a commitment to God's vision.

3. THE VISION IS DISTRIBUTED TO THE CHURCH

The plans and purposes of God are not complete when they are only delivered to the pastor. There's more. The minister has a responsibility to distribute the vision to the church.

Here's how that is accomplished:

- Pastors must insure that persons under their leadership are apprised of God's plans for that particular flock.
- The local church members must know that the vision is broad and requires the effort of *all* believers to effectively maintain its progression.
- The pastor must keep what the Lord has revealed constantly before the people. That's how it will be understood and supported.
- The vision must be made plain.

*I will stand upon my watch, and set me upon
the tower, and will watch to see what he will say
unto me, and what I shall answer when I am reproved.
And the Lord answered me, and said, Write the vision,
and make it plain upon tables, that he may run that
readeth it. For the vision is yet for an appointed
time, but at the end it shall speak, and not lie:*

though it tarry, wait for it; because it will
surely come, it will not tarry.

HABAKKUK 2:1-3

What the Lord has in store for a particular congregation is not what God envisions for the entire Body of Christ. It is only a portion of His plan.

Only through fellowship with other ministries are we able to become familiar with additional aspects of God's work being carried out.

IT IS SPIRIT-REVEALED

The entire vision is in the mind of God. Since He is the Master and the Creator of all things, He alone sees the picture in its entirety. It is vitally important, however, that what He knows – and what He desires us to know – is progressively revealed to His people. This is achieved through the Holy Spirit.

But as it is written, Eye hath not seen, nor
ear heard, neither have entered into the heart
of man, the things which God hath prepared for
them that love him. But God hath revealed them
unto us by His Spirit: for the Spirit searcheth all
things, yea, the deep things of God.

1 CORINTHIANS 2:9-10

The presence of the Holy Spirit in the pastor's life will not only bring a recognition of God's vision; it will be accompanied by a plan to be used in its implementation. If the revelation is not clear, the man of God should go before the Lord in fasting and prayer to receive a clear understanding of what the Lord is saying.

Here is the danger. A misunderstood revelation can result in a misguided vision. The Holy Spirit provides the *data* to us in a manner that can be clearly understood by the one to whom it is directed. If there is difficulty in comprehending the revelation, the problem lies with us, not the Holy Spirit.

> *A misunderstood revelation can result in a misguided vision.*

THE LAITY'S RESPONSIBILITY

The vision is also revealed to believers by the Holy Spirit. That is why the laity, like pastors, must continually walk in the Spirit.

To comment, "I understand what the pastor is saying," is only part of the process. Believers who truly receive the vision not only embrace it, but a commitment will be sparked within them to support, endorse and defend it.

Until church members identify with God's vision through their pastor to the extent of giving it their full loyalty, they have not received it.

If believers know their pastor is a Godly person with a

solid ministerial history, then they should follow the *God* in him – without resistance to some parts of the process they may not understand. I am not promoting a walk that ignores logic, rather a walk by faith in God and in the shepherd of the flock.

> *It is through the Holy Spirit that both the minister and church members receive what is being given.*

Believers need to be reminded that pastors are the *vision carriers*. God's revelation is given to pastors who, in turn, impart it to the laity. It is through the Holy Spirit that both the minister and church members receive what is being presented.

IT IS SPIRIT-LED

Before Christ ascended to heaven, as He comforted the disciples, He indicated that when the Holy Spirit came, He would lead them into what was true.

> *Howbeit when he, the Spirit of truth, is come, he will guide you into all truth: for he shall not speak of himself: but whatsoever he shall hear, that shall he speak: and he will shew you things to come.*
> JOHN 16:13

This is a dynamic function of the ministry of the Holy

38

Spirit. He not only reveals the path we are to take, He faithfully stays by our side – leading and guiding us into a revelation of God's will and God's Word.

A STRONG LEADING

More than once I have received a revelation of a particular portion of the vision, but did not know when it would be achieved.

Earlier in this chapter I described the physical effort that went into the establishment of our Community Support Center. It was much more than an idea. The project was a portion of the vision God had given me for our church.

At the time, I felt a strong leading to immediately move forward, yet there was no room in our facility to establish such a center. I prayed, "Lord, why would You give me this vision and leave me perplexed concerning how to fulfill it?"

I soon discovered that the Lord did not cause me to be confused. It was my fault. I *became* uncertain in my own mind while trying to figure it out.

I was concerned about the possible location, the enormous task and the lack of finances. These things, however, were never an issue with God.

Not many days after the revelation, the Holy Spirit turned my attention to a building situated next to our church facility. The structure was occupied by a local bar that was starting to lose money. The man who leased the facility and ran the tavern had continually complained, "The church is hurting my business."

Because our ministry had become strong in the

community, his customers were going down the street to another bar because they didn't want to disrespect the church. At one point the saloon manager had even threatened to slash the tires of anyone who attended our services and parked in front of his establishment.

During these days, the Lord revealed to me that the saloon could be used to house the Community Support Center.

WE CLAIMED IT!

In the middle of a Sunday night service, while I was preaching, the Holy Spirit led me to say, "I want everyone in this auditorium to turn toward that bar. We are going to stretch out our hands and claim it in the Name of Jesus."

That's exactly what we did!

Within two weeks the property owner of the building called me to see if we were interested in purchasing it. The bar occupant was significantly in arrears and about to be evicted. It wasn't long until we acquired the building.

> *"We are going to stretch out our hands and claim it in the Name of Jesus."*

The Community Support center was the direct result of the leading of the Holy Spirit. Everything was on hold until our congregation claimed that building by faith.

Again and again I have seen how the Spirit leads us in

our living, giving, decision making, planning and spiritual achievement. When both the pastor and laity follow the leading of the Holy Spirit, it brings harmony and assures the advancement and fulfillment of God's vision.

IT IS SPIRIT-EMPOWERED

When the Lord begins to work, Satan is not only annoyed, he begins to harass. However, if heaven's plan is to be realized, the forces of evil must be overcome by those in the pulpit and those in the pew.

To win the battle, we must be properly empowered.

But ye shall receive power after that the Holy Ghost is come upon you: and ye shall be witnesses unto me both in Jerusalem, and in all Judea, and in Samaria, and unto the uttermost part of the earth.
ACTS 1:8

The Holy Spirit is the source of our strength. He allows us to manifest both the Fruit of The Spirit and the Gifts of the Spirit. They enable us to achieve God's purpose.

But the fruit of the Spirit is love, joy, peace, longsuffering, gentleness, goodness, faith, meekness, temperance: against such there is no law.
GALATIANS 5:23

This one verse reveals that the Holy Spirit enables us:
■ To love God's vision.

41

- To be joyful in all of our activities that advance it.
- To be peaceful or calm in the face of every adversity.
- To suffer long and endure affliction and hardship.
- To be gentle or kind as we relate to and interact with others involved in God's plan.
- To be good, reflecting proper Godly qualities.
- To exercise faith in the Lord for the progression and fulfillment of His will.
- To be meek, practicing patience and mildness in all our interactions.
- To be temperate or moderate, showing restraint and avoiding excess as we engage in the vision.

For to one is given by the Spirit the word
of wisdom; to another the word of knowledge
by the same Spirit; to another faith by the same
Spirit; to another the gifts of healing by the same
Spirit; to another the working of miracles; to
another discerning of spirits; to another
divers kinds of tongues; to another the
interpretation of tongues.
1 CORINTHIANS 12:8-11

The Gifts of the Spirit are for today! I know first hand how they give mighty power to the church.

~

Vision is not the result of man's foresight or human creativity. It is determined by God, and, through the power of the Holy Spirit, delivered to pastors and distributed to the church.

CHAPTER THREE

~

SIX ESSENTIAL REQUIREMENTS

One of the most powerful words in the Bible has only two letters – and appears over 1,500 times. That word is "if."

You can open the scriptures from Genesis to Revelation and find there are conditions and requirements for receiving God's favor. For example, Deuteronomy 28 details the great blessings the Lord wants to give to His people. However, when you read the first two verses, you discover that important word "if."

*And it shall come to pass, if thou shalt hearken
diligently unto the voice of the LORD thy God,
to observe and to do all his commandments which I command thee this day, that the LORD thy God will set thee
on high above all nations of the earth: And all these*

*blessings shall come on thee, and overtake thee, if thou
shalt hearken unto the voice of the LORD thy God.*
DEUTERONOMY 28:1-2

If you will observe and do His commandments. *If* you
will hearken unto the voice of the Lord, He will open wide
the windows of heaven.

There are also conditions for receiving God's vision. In
this chapter we are going to discover six of them.

REQUIREMENT NUMBER ONE:

LOVE

When Jesus was questioned by a Pharisee lawyer
concerning which commandment was the greatest, here was
His response:

*Jesus saith unto him, Thou shalt love the
Lord thy God with all thy heart, and with
all thy soul, and with all thy mind.*

MATTHEW 22:37

The answer was not only vital during the time of Christ,
it is crucial today. Our love for the Lord should be *total*. He
is our God and Creator and should receive the very best we
can offer from every area of our lives. It should be to such
a degree that *Kingdom* business takes priority over our own
– so strong that His cause receives the highest commitment
of our abilities and resources.

We must worship the Author of Love so completely that we will work untiringly to promote the fulfillment of His vision.

Our love must flourish and grow to the point that we can identify with the words of Paul:

> *"What? Know ye not that your body is the temple of the Holy Ghost which is in you which ye have of God, and ye are not your own?"*
> 1 CORINTHIANS 6:19

The verse that follows confirms that you and I have been *"bought with a price"* - the shed blood of Jesus Christ. And you must *"glorify God in your body, and in your spirit, which are God's* (v.20). Our love for the Father must be so passionate that we willingly yield our bodies as living sacrifices unto Him.

Our love for the Father must be so passionate that we willingly yield our bodies as living sacrifices unto Him.

THE STANDARD

As possessors of the Holy Spirit, which empowers us, we are able to love as God prescribes. The standard was stated by Paul to the Corinthians:

47

*Charity suffereth long, and is kind; charity
envieth not; charity vaunteth no itself, is not
puffed up. Doth not behave itself unseemly, seeketh
not her own, is not easily provoked, thinketh no evil;
Rejoiceth not in iniquity, but rejoiceth in the truth;
Beareth all things, believeth all things, hopeth all
things, endureth all things. Charity never faileth;
but whether there be prophecies, they shall fail;
whether there be tongues, they shall cease; whether
there be knowledge, it shall vanish away.*

1 CORINTHIANS 13:4-8

It is a principle of God's Word *that in order to love others, you must first love yourself.* Jesus declared, *"...Thou shalt love thy neighbor as thyself"* (Matthew 22:39).

~

*In order to love
others, you must
first love yourself.*

By knowing how to properly value ourselves, we gain the experience and knowledge necessary to esteem others. This is a strong bonding factor in the Body of Christ. Love unites us and makes it possible for God's vision to be advanced.

I've watched believers who attend church services and even have a specific role in ministry, yet they don't reach their potential in the church because they fail to love according to the Word. They are the ones written about by John: *"He that loveth not knoweth not God; for God is love"*(1 John 4:8).

NO RETALIATION

During my years as a pastor, my deep love for the Lord has been my strength. With great disappointment, I must admit that a few church members have falsely accused me and with stinging words have sought to inflict pain on me and my wife in their attempt to destroy the ministry.

Later, some of those same individuals have come to me in their hour of need. Because of the love God poured into me, I was able to rise above their past actions and give them the help they required. Eventually some stopped being a detriment and became great blessings to the Body of Christ. The love and nurturing they received caused them to recapture the vision.

It is only through God's amazing grace and boundless love that we are able to forgive and treat people according to the Word – not retaliating for the way we may have been treated.

Beloved, let us love one another: for
love is of God; and everyone that loveth
is born of God, and knoweth God.
1 JOHN 4:7

REQUIREMENT NUMBER TWO:
PRAYER

God's vision is advanced by an army of believers

marching on its knees. Through prayer we commune with our Heavenly Father.

Although we don't like to admit it, the devil is often quite successful at disrupting our fellowship with God. Just look at the small attendance that shows up for a prayer service and you'll understand what I mean. This is true whether the congregation meets in a storefront building or a mega-church worshiping in a multi-million dollar facility. Sunday morning services are filled to capacity and the parking lots are jammed with automobiles, yet when a prayer meeting is announced, sadly, the room is full of empty seats.

> *Church members who fail to talk with the Lord are operating far below their potential.*

This should come as no surprise when we conclude that the average church is mostly comprised of believers who have weak prayer lives.

Church members who fail to talk with the Lord are operating far below their potential. Their *prayerlessness* is the measure by which God's vision is being hindered.

The Lord does not appreciate an on-again-off-again prayer life, based on the urgency of our current needs. The Bible tells us to *"Pray without ceasing"* (1 Thessalonians 5:17). I am convinced more than ever that it must become a consistent activity of every Christian.

IT'S NECESSARY

Open the Word and you'll discover that prayer is a necessary ingredient for every child of God – whether a seasoned saint or a new convert.

1. Abraham prayed for Sodom (Genesis 18:23-33).
2. Moses prayed for plagues to come upon Pharaoh's Egypt (Exodus 8-12).
3. Joshua prayed for extended daylight (Joshua 10:12).
4. Gideon prayed for a sign (Judges 6:36-40).
5. Samson prayed for strength (Judges 16:28-31).
6. David prayed for forgiveness (Psalm 51).
7. Solomon prayed for wisdom (1 Kings 3:5-9).
8. Elijah prayed for fire (I Kings 18:36-37).
9. Elisha prayed for spiritual vision for his servant 2 Kings 6:17).
10. Hezekiah prayed for a lengthened life (2 Kings 20:1-3).
11. Disciples of Jesus prayed for boldness in witnessing (Acts 4:24-30).
12. Jesus prayed (Matthew 26:26-46).

Seeking God was imperative in each of these lives, and is equally essential today.

ADVANCING GOD'S KINGDOM

Scripture declares that the "...*effectual fervent prayer of a righteous man availeth much*" (James 5:16).

If the health of your church were measured by the prayer life of its members, how would it rank in God's eyes? Before *fervent* prayer is promoted, it would be good to start with prayer of *any* kind.

We are in an untenable position when the Lord instructs us to pray without ceasing, and the majority of believers have virtually no prayer life at all.

How can we achieve what God intends if our personal communication with the Lord is neglected or even omitted?

Satan knows that the flesh has no desire to pray. And when Christians don't fellowship with the Lord, they are following their flesh rather than the Spirit of God. What an indictment against the church!

If we are going to advance God's Kingdom, we must intensify our prayer lives – and inform non-praying believers of the importance of spending time with the Lord.

THE BENEFITS

Prayer keeps the vision moving forward:

- It reveals the will of God (Luke 11:9-10).
- It keeps us from sin (Matthew 26:41).
- It defeats the devil (Luke 22:32).
- It brings the impartation of wisdom (James 1:5).
- It produces the impossible (Matthew 21:22).
- It sends forth laborers (Matthew 9:38).
- It restores backsliders (James 5:16).
- It produces the peace of God (Philippians 4:6-7).

Let me encourage you to become *diligent* in prayer. It's

the secret ingredient of helping to fulfill God's purpose for His church.

REQUIREMENT NUMBER THREE:
COMMITMENT

Commit thy way unto the Lord; trust
also in him; and he shall bring it to pass.

PSALM 37:5

The key to receiving what God desires for you is found in *commitment* and *trust*. However, you can't be dedicated to any and every cause that happens to cross your path. You need a *proper* commitment – to the truth, to the Almighty, His Kingdom and His vision.

Countless problems arise in the Body of Christ because of well-meaning Christians

> *God expects an untiring effort, plus our willingness to fight the forces of Satan.*

who live by the motto, "I'll do it my way!" It's not *your* way that counts, rather God's purpose that must be the object of your loyalty.

To see the Father's will revealed in our lives there are two important requirements: *work* and *warfare*. God expects an untiring effort, plus our willingness to fight the forces of Satan.

These two crucial elements demand people who are totally dedicated to *"press toward the mark"* (Philippians 3:14).

Let me remind you that God's plans do not instantly appear as a flashing neon sign or an illuminated highway billboard. They are revealed progressively as we stay committed, fight the enemy and work unceasingly to help fulfill the promises of God.

AT ANY COST!

Heros of history are ordinary people with extraordinary passion. They are also like you and me – with unique interests, likes, dislikes and desires. What sets them apart, however, is the fact that they centered their existence on one particular objective – and began to strive for it with great intensity and dedication.

Often their commitment meant death.

- Peter was crucified.
- Paul was beheaded.
- Stephen was stoned.
- Ignatius, Bishop of Antioch, was thrown to wild beasts.
- Polycarp was burned on a woodpile.
- Justin Martin was beaten and beheaded.

The list of Christian martyrs continues to this very day, with missionaries still being tortured and put to death for the cause of Christ. They sacrifice their lives because of the depth of their love for the Savior.

What about the commitment of those in a local church? Many fall by the wayside because they are only dedicated to their private agendas.

> *Our thoughts, actions and deeds will reflect our resolve in carrying out the particular assignment the Lord has given to us.*

What would you do if you were about to be fed to a hungry lion, burned at the stake, or even beheaded? Would you maintain your allegiance to God, or would you waver and run for your life?

Commitment is necessary in the life of every believer. It is needed for the following three reasons:

First: To establish our thoughts.

Having *"the mind of Christ"* (1 Corinthians 2:16) requires a disciplined study of the Word and daily spending time in the Lord's presence. As a result, our thoughts, actions and deeds will reflect our resolve in carrying out the particular assignment the Lord has given to us.

> *Search me, O God, and know my heart:*
> *try me, and know my thoughts.*
> PSALM 139:23

Second: To Be Molded By God

If we are going to be effectively used of the Lord, we

must allow Him to form and shape us. Thank God, we are not who we used to be – and certainly not who we *will* be. Only our Heavenly Father knows the person we will ultimately become. Therefore, He must mold us into His instrument to help complete His divine tasks on this earth.

It may come as a shock when we discover that some of the things we dislike in life are the very components being used to *form* us, *inform* us, and *conform* us to the vision.

> ◠
>
> *Our commitment is established when we become pliable clay in the Potter's hands.*

If we are stubborn and do not yield to the life-shaping hands of God, we will not be able to overcome the opposition that will arrive because of our identification with His cause. Refusal to accept God's life-changing process will cause us to fail in the fulfillment of His objectives. Our commitment is established when we become pliable clay in the Potter's hands.

If He is not allowed to pattern our lives, we will not be able to endure the suffering, sacrifice and persecution that may accompany being active in God's service.

Third: To Have Ways That Please God

Trust in the Lord with all thine heart; and lean not unto thine own understanding. In all thy ways acknowledge him, and he shall direct thy paths.

PROVERBS 3:5-6

When our daily activities please the Lord, they reflect the fact that we trust in Him, lean upon Him and acknowledge Him in all our ways. What is the result? He will guide our Christian walk.

The steps of a good man are ordered by the Lord: and he delighteth in his way.
PSALM 37:23

We honor the Lord when we allow Him to direct our journey – one footprint at a time. When we acknowledge His leadership, we remain in His will and stay on course.

Without total dedication to the Lord, I would have stumbled and perhaps even *failed* in my efforts to advance the clear picture of the future He unveiled to me.

Through the power of the Holy Spirit and our love for the Lord we can achieve a level of commitment that will assure the completion of our given task.

REQUIREMENT NUMBER FOUR:
SUBMISSION

Submit yourselves therefore to God.
Resist the devil, and he will flee from you.
JAMES 4:7

It is a Biblical requirement that we must fully yield our lives to the Lord. The submitted Christian is an *obedient* Christian.

By faith, we must place ourselves in the hands of God so

He can receive the greatest quality and talent from our lives. I constantly see the difficulty many believers experience in submitting to God. They know He exists, that He is all-powerful and unequaled, that He knows all and is present everywhere. They understand this – and more. Yet, they will not surrender themselves totally to the Father. Obviously, the pull of the flesh is so powerful they continually lean on their own selfish cravings rather than obeying the desires of the Lord.

~

To properly identify with God's vision, we must have our priorities in order.

To properly identify with God's vision, we must have our priorities in order. It is an essential element in the process of submission.

But seek ye first the kingdom of God, and his righteousness: and all these things shall be added unto you.
MATTHEW 6:33

Jesus, in His Sermon on the Mount, made it clear that we must place God first – above all else. This means that we must start by presenting our self-will, our ways and our actions to Him. Without submission we cannot walk in a manner worthy of our calling.

Yielding to the Father is a prerequisite to the other forms of submission. Let's look at them.

SUBMISSION TO SPIRITUAL LEADERSHIP

Obey them that have the rule over you, and submit yourselves: for they watch for your souls, as they that must give account, that they may do it with joy, and not with grief: for that is unprofitable for you.

HEBREWS 13:17

One of the important themes of this book is to understand the role of pastors in the fulfillment of what God has designed. In the last chapter we discussed the commission of ministers in the *distribution* of the heavenly plan. Their effectiveness can be measured by the extent of submission evident in the laity.

Remember, *the vision is advanced when the members of the church submit themselves to the God-given authority of the pastor.* Those who ignore this admonition not only disobey the Father, but also place themselves in the position of opposing God's program.

- They are disobedient to God because He commands believers to obey and be subject to pastors who are in His will.
- They are out of step with the vision and, therefore, out of step with the Lord.
- They align themselves with everyone and everything that opposes God's plans.
- They close the door to the blessings of the Lord.

- They open themselves to the attack and destruction of the enemy.
- They prevent spiritual growth and development in their lives.
- They are removed from the benefits that God provides through pastors in relation to His vision.
- They are bad examples for other believers.
- They are not effective witnesses for the Lord.
- They lack the power and the ability to engage in a Godly walk.
- They promote disobedience and non-submission.
- They encourage division and disunity in the Body of Christ.
- They will reap an undesirable harvest for their deeds.

Just because God has given pastors rule and authority over believers under their care, does not mean ministers are not accountable for their actions. Shepherds of the flock are responsible for watching over the souls of every church member – and must give an account to God for how they do so.

Church members have an obligation too. Disobedience can rob the pastor of joy and promote grief. What is the result? Without doubt, the effectiveness of the pastor will be eroded. When ministers of the Gospel are grieving, their role in fulfilling God's purpose is negatively affected – and the vision itself is diminished.

What a difference it makes when we live according to the Father's plan.

SUBMISSION TO OTHERS

I fees sorry for the person who says, "If they're not going to follow my suggestions, I'm leaving this church."

God has other ideas. He calls for all believers to be like-minded — submitted one to another.

> *What a difference it makes when we live according to the Father's plan.*

> *Likewise ye younger, submit yourselves unto the elder. Yea, all of you be subject one to another, and be clothed with humility: for God resisteth the proud, and giveth grace to the humble.*
> 1 PETER 5:5

The question we must ask is not "How will this benefit me?" Rather, we should inquire, "How will this edify the mission God has for His Kingdom and for this church?"

Many persons are involved in the harvest. They represent varying educational and economic backgrounds, plus all races, creeds, and nationalities. Yet, thank the Lord, all are equal in His sight.

In God's Kingdom, things are achieved in a spiritual

manner – not according to the policies and procedures found in business or industry. For example, He appoints us based upon the sincerity of our walk with Him. This means that a person's resume may be lacking in education or experience, yet because of their spiritual walk, the Lord will give them an awesome assignment.

He appoints us based on the sincerity of our walk with Him.

I'm sure you can see the difficulty of a church member who is a CEO with a Master's degree submitting themselves to a woman who takes in laundry. It punctures their pride! The Lord, however, doesn't appoint spiritual leaders based on their position in society, rather on the sincerity of their hearts.

REASONS FOR NOT SUBMITTING

Here are six reasons many refuse to obey God's command regarding this matter:

1. Some do not submit because they think too highly of themselves.

The person who has problems yielding to others may be suffering from an inflated ego. They need to remember that *"God resisteth the proud"* (1 Peter 5:5).

For I say, through the grace given unto me, to every man that is among you, not to think of himself more highly than he ought to think: but to think soberly, according as God hath dealt to every man the measure of faith.

ROMANS 12:3

God is no respecter of persons; He loves us all. We are not suddenly superior because we have accomplished more than others.

2. **Some do not submit because they are not of the same mind.**
   "Be of the same mind one towards another..." (Romans 12:16).
3. **Some are not peaceful.**
   "If it be possible, as much as lieth in you, live peaceably with all men" (Romans 12:18).
4. **Some are overcome by sin.**
   "Be not overcome of evil, but overcome evil with good" (Romans 12:21).
5. **Some do not have good prayer lives.**
   "Rejoicing in hope, patient in tribulation; continuing instant in prayer" (Romans 12:12).
6. **Some are spiritually weak.**
   "Finally, my brethren, be strong in the Lord, and in the power of his might" (Eph. 6:10).

BLOCKING PROGRESS

When believers do not submit to one another, God's work is harmed:

- It prevents proper training or communication of needed information.
- It causes division and strife.
- It promotes disrespect.
- It provides a basis for the development and continuance of pride.
- It sets a poor example for new converts.
- It hinders the development of informed, Godly believers.
- It prevents the exchange of the vital knowledge that is needed to keep God's dream alive.

The Father's command that we are to *"be subject one to another, and be clothed with humility"* should be stored in our souls and demonstrated by our actions.

REQUIREMENT NUMBER FIVE:
DETERMINATION

For I am persuaded, that neither death,
nor life, nor powers, nor things present, nor things
to come, nor height, nor depth, nor any other creature,
shall be able to separate us from the love of God,
which is in Christ Jesus our Lord.
ROMANS 8:38-39

What a reflection of the depth of determination found

in Paul the Apostle! It is also a barometer of what our level of resolve should be.

Like Paul, we must possess a purpose-driven faith. He was fully persuaded to stay close to the Lord, whether in life or death. He would not

> *Like Paul, we must possess a purpose-driven faith.*

be sidetracked or detoured by outside forces. *Nothing* was about to come between himself and the love of God.

Is that your prayer? It had better be, since the devil and his forces will test your very soul. Satan wants nothing more than to demolish God's plan for the ages.

INTENSITY IS REQUIRED

Determination is affected by desire. A person dying of thirst in a hot, arid desert will push on relentlessly in search of an oasis. The craving for water, and for life itself, causes us to call on our hidden resources to survive.

I believe God's vision is being neglected, in part because so many believers have lost their intense desire for the achievement of the purposes of the Father. It is sad to see so many striving for material possessions - homes, cars, clothing, furniture, and more. They go to great lengths and sacrifice much to accumulate their "want list" - even if it means working two or three jobs. Some are so engrossed in money-making activities they have little time for their families, and even less for the Lord.

Can you imagine what would happen if Christians would demonstrate that same urgency to see God's mission for His church realized?

Pure determination produces action – even if it is a solo effort. We will push toward what the Lord has directed, even if no one else does.

Our objective should be to seek a level of dedication that will cause us to do all we can without leaning and depending upon others. Too often believers find themselves stagnant – going nowhere – because they have no one to help them. They say, "I am only one person, and what can one individual do?"

- Remember Noah! He was only one solitary man, yet the Lord used him to build an ark that eventually brought the salvation of himself and his family.
- Joseph was one man in Egypt that God used to preserve the Jewish nation.
- Paul was one man that God chose to evangelize the world during his lifetime.

With "true grit" that is inspired by the principles found in the Word, we will fight the good fight – even if those who started with us lay down their swords and shields along the way.

"I WON'T LET GO!"

Genuine determination is durable; it has a "I will not

SIX ESSENTIAL REQUIREMENTS

quit – I will not be discouraged" attitude.

In Genesis 32, Jacob wrestled the Lord until daybreak. He was so intent on being blessed by God that he engaged in a hand to hand struggle, using his physical strength to obtain what he desired.

Your tenacity can allow you to go the distance – to hang in there, no matter what.

This heart-driven passion overcomes opposition that is sometimes manifested as failure, disappointment and a lack of assistance. Your tenacity can allow you to go the distance – to hang in there, no matter what – even in the presence of harsh resistance and suffering.

When combined with faith, your dedication will bring remarkable results. Jacob wrestled with such a deep belief that the Lord touched and disjointed his thigh. Even then, Jacob said, *"I will not let thee go, except thou bless me"* (Genesis 32:26)

He was so persistent that the Lord said to him:

> *Thy name shall be called no more Jacob, but*
> *Israel: for as a prince hast thou power with*
> *God and with men, and hast prevailed.*
> GENESIS 32:28

Determination achieves victories in skirmishes that

could have easily been losses. It grabs defeat by the collar, looks it straight in the eyes and says, "There is no room for you here!"

We must seize every challenge and utter those same words. God's vision must move forward.

REQUIREMENT NUMBER SIX:
PATIENCE

As Kingdom citizens, we experience many wondrous days – even though we often endure our share of adversity. At times, however, it may seem the Lord is not concerned about our trials. I've heard people complain, "Why does it take God so long to answer my prayers?"

> *"Why does it take God so long to answer my prayers?"*

We quickly forget the words of the psalmist, who said:

> *I waited patiently for the LORD: and*
> *he inclined unto me, and heard my cry.*
> PSALM 40:1

Patience is a key element in the fulfillment of God's program:

68

- It is the ability to calmly bear trouble without complaining.
- It is steadfastness despite opposition and difficulty.
- It is a cheerful, fortified endurance.

We mentioned earlier that the progression of God's plan will not be achieved without warfare. As the battles intensify, there will be moments when we want the Lord to move immediately on our behalf. We've become a quick-delivery, drive-through, instant society.

Well, our Father is not always going to respond when we snap our fingers. So what do we do? We must learn to patiently and prayerfully wait on Him.

HE WAITED

Paul refers to the Lord as our *"God of patience"* (Romans 15:5). He carefully deals with all of creation on His own time schedule. The Holy Scriptures record events in the lives of many believers that reflect God's gracious patience with humanity. On numerous occasions He was rejected, disregarded, forgotten, and even replaced by idols, yet He rarely rushed to judgment – giving the people time to repent.

Just as God exhibits restraint, so must we. The work we are involved in is His. If *anyone* wants to see it fulfilled, the Lord certainly does.

Relax! Don't be in such a big hurry:

69

- Prayers that have not been answered, will be.
- Resources that have not been delivered, will appear.
- He alone can see the "big picture" – and He sets the timetable.

Our personal prayers and concerns are welcomed by the Lord, but He must consider them as they relate to the welfare of His entire Kingdom. Viewed from our narrow vantage point, we conclude, "Now is the time for the answer."

His heavenly panoramic view, however, could dictate otherwise. Regardless, we must practice patience – calmly braving the current difficulties and maintaining hope.

For whatsoever things were written aforetime were written for our learning, that we through patience and comfort of the scriptures might have hope.
ROMANS 15:4

God will perform all that He says He will do, but in His own way and on His own schedule. What the Lord envisions will be achieved and if we adhere to it, there is no way we can fail. Staying with His plan makes us a participant, and, as a result, our success is personally guaranteed by God.

DON'T GIVE UP

We must also exercise patience with one another.

Now the God of patience and consolation grant you to be likeminded one toward another according to Christ Jesus.

ROMANS 15:5

Many Christian friendships unravel and fall apart because believers do not practice forbearance with one another. We are counseled to *"be patient toward all men"* (1 Thessalonians 5:14). Instead, we continually see church members doing just the opposite.

They give up on each other over small matters such as negative comments, money owed, a broken promise, a missed appointment, relationship problems, to name a few. The Lord's vision is far greater than our petty differences. We can't give precedence to personal feelings and desires that promote division. I have seen highly skilled believers refuse to utilize their talents because someone has said or done something to offend them.

> *The Lord's vision is far greater than our petty differences.*

To stop working for the Lord because of another person's negative actions is to align oneself with the enemy. Display patience with those who ruffle your feathers and, by all means, forgive them. Then joyfully continue in the activities to which the Lord has directed you.

WHAT ABOUT YOU?

Not only must we be patient with others – but also with ourselves. As born again followers of the Savior, we must seek to know our capabilities.

I have observed church members who have unrealistic hopes and dreams because of an improper self-evaluation. If we rate our potential too high, our expectations will be impossible to achieve. This also means that we will expect to do things in an unrealistic time-frame. When that happens, we become disillusioned and feel that we should have already reached our goal.

Continual failure has caused many to throw in the towel. What is the solution? When believers fail, they must dust off their frustration and start moving forward so that the Lord's work will not be jeopardized. Instead of increasing our blood pressure and getting upset with ourselves, we must take the matter to the Lord in prayer.

Patience is vital in vision fulfillment:

- It keeps us calm in the midst of difficulties and hardship.
- It enables us to wait on the Lord and to be content with His time-frames.
- It promotes peace as we interact with other believers in the fulfillment of vision functions.
- It enables us to resist frustration, discouragement, and disappointment.
- It helps us to maintain an active and lively hope.
- It empowers us to possess the promises of God.

- It keeps us focused and fortified in trying times.
- It helps us to stay grounded in the Lord so that we are not easily moved.
- It keeps us cheerful and in good spirits.
- It maintains the sincerity in our worship and praise.

~

Now it is time for an honest appraisal of ourselves. Are we meeting the Father's requirements? Are we putting God's love into daily practice? Are we men and women of fervent prayer? Are we totally committed to the vision? Do we practice humble submission? Do we possess a determined faith? Are we demonstrating patience?

With God's help, I trust your answer to each of these questions will become a resounding "Yes!"

CHAPTER FOUR

~

"AND HE GAVE PASTORS"

Like many who accept the call to the ministry, I was not fully aware of the challenges that were ahead.

For years, I had been faithful to my own pastor and had carefully observed him in his devotion and performance of his pastoral duties. Somehow, I thought that my years of involvement in the church had prepared me for the step I was about to take.

What a shock was waiting for me! It did not take long to discover how totally unprepared I was for leading a church. I had been standing before a congregation for five years when the Lord revealed to me, "Now I am ready to start making you into a pastor."

"Start?" I questioned. "What have I been doing for the past five years?"

In prayer, I realized that my experience to that point

was only a training course.

THE VITAL LINK

The role of the pastor in carrying out God's purpose cannot be overemphasized. The position has been ordained by the Almighty and is the vital link that connects born again Christians to the Father's objectives.

It's a three-step process:

> *First: The Lord births in a pastor the portion of the vision that He will use them to achieve.*
>
> *Second: The man or woman of God must distribute the Lord's plan to those in the local church.*
>
> *Third: The pastor must maintain a position of leadership to see the mandate move forward.*

A minister is accountable to God for carrying out His directives.

The revelation is given to them by God through the working of the Holy Spirit and they immediately become responsible for the assignment given to them. A minister is accountable to God for carrying out His directives.

TEN EXPECTATIONS

How do pastors fit into the Lord's plan? Here are ten

reasons and requisites:

1. They were created by God to be vision carriers.
2. They receive the revelation from God.
3. They are responsible for the distribution of the Father's plan to those under their leadership.
4. They perform key roles in the process and must be sure that they clearly understand what God has said to them.
5. They must keep the vision before laity, and be examples of how to properly relate to it.
6. They must lead the implementation of the various portions of the assignment and assure adherence to God's directives.
7. They must lead the warfare against the enemies that come against God's program, and train other believers to engage in spiritual warfare.
8. They must insure that all of the supporting resources are properly managed.
9. They must (when necessary) reprove, rebuke, and exhort others involved in fulfilling the mission.
10. They must live in the presence of God so they can continually receive revelation of the vision.

TIMES ARE DIFFERENT

Changes in our culture have proven difficult for many in the ministry. In previous generations, people seemed to exhibit a far deeper respect for members of the clergy. I know it was true for me.

As early as I can remember, I was introduced to the church by my parents. They were strong Christians who believed in sincere service to God and we attended church at least three to four times every week. Most Sundays my parents packed lunch for the family and we stayed all day.

What stands out in my mind, though, is the respect my parents had for the pastor. This esteem was also manifested in the lives of many other believers. When the pastor spoke, the congregation listened with a "Thus saith the Lord" attitude.

Over the years, however, the level of admiration has changed. We have experienced the widely-publicized fall of well-known evangelists, and the secular media has had a field day, gleefully disclosing the faults and failures of ministers. As a result, questions and clouds have hovered over the clergy. They wonder, "Is my pastor like that?"

This loss of confidence in spiritual leadership is exactly what Satan has been scheming so long to achieve. He knows that if he can destroy trust in those who stand behind the pulpits of our land he can significantly reduce the effectiveness of Christian efforts.

Despite these temporary setbacks, I am convinced the church will be ultimately triumphant.

NEGATIVE ATTITUDES

The image of the Christian church portrayed by the media has been extremely damaging. It has shaped public opinion and has carved deep scars in the attitude of people toward the things of God.

I have personally experienced some of these negative sentiments. Recently, I was asked by a stranger, "What is your occupation?"

When I responded, "I am a pastor," his demeanor changed. Almost immediately, he began asking a series of questions: "What make of car do you drive? What kind of house do your live in? Does your church pay you well?"

I knew instantly that his attitude had been shaped by the reports of journalists and circulated by word-of-mouth. And now I was being interrogated.

> *It's easy to understand why some pastors lose heart and feel like turning to some other profession.*

It's easy to understand why some pastors lose heart and feel like turning to some other profession. After all, people will not follow leadership they cannot trust. They may stay in the church, yet will distance themselves from God's appointed servant.

THE FACTS

The following research was reported in the book, PASTORS AT RISK, by H. B. London, Jr., and Neil B. Weisman.[1]

1. Two out of three adult Americans (67%) say there

is no such thing as absolute truth.

2. The United States population has increased 41 percent since 1960. During that time there has been a 560 percent increase in violent crimes; a 419 percent increase in illegitimate births, a quadrupling in divorce rates; a tripling of the percentage of children living in single parent homes; more than 200 percent increase in teenage suicides; and a drop of almost 80 points in SAT scores.

3. One leadership magazine reported:
   - 94% of pastors surveyed feel pressured to have an ideal family.
   - 24% have received or are receiving marital counseling.
   - 38% are dissatisfied with the level of sexual intimacy in their marriages, and pastors report 16 percent of their spouses are dissatisfied, which 69 percent blame on the busy schedule, 54 percent on their spouses schedule, and 35 percent on frequent night church meetings.

4. 12% of ministers reported they were depressed "often" or "always" in their ministry.

5. 70% of the pastors indicated that their compensation contributed to the conflict in their marriage.

6. 22% of pastors felt forced to supplement their church income.

7. Over 40% of the single staff pastors and 33% of senior ministers, for a total of 78% felt they were

underpaid.

8. 75% of the surveyed clergy report experiencing periods of major distress.

9. 33% reported that they had seriously considered leaving the ministry.

10. An estimated 20% of the nation's 300,000 clergy suffer from long-term stress.

The first statistic indicates that many people are moving from Biblical truth. As a result, both the church and world are experiencing spiritual and moral decay.

An estimated 20% of the nation's 300,000 clergy suffer from long-term stress.

The conditions reported in this research – plus many more – deeply affect the life of the pastor. However, despite these realities, dedicated men and women of God delight in performing their spiritual duties.

THE "WATCHING"

The Bible is crystal clear regarding how members of the church are to relate to their pastor. The admonition to *"Obey them that have rule over you"* (Hebrews 13:17) is not written about submitting to governmental authority. It specifically refers to how the laity is to respond to those who *"watch for your souls"* (v.17).

Though a church member may be intellectually brilliant

and economically prosperous, he still needs the "watching" of a pastor.

When believers come under the leadership of a minister, that pastor has the God-given responsibility of watching for their souls. Church members need to realize the importance of the "watching" that is the duty of their pastors.

JUST ANOTHER OPINION?

Every minister of the Gospel has an obligation to speak the Word of God - and people are to obey that spoken word. In family and personal matters, the counsel of the pastor must not be seen as "just another opinion." A spiritual leader who is in tune with God, speaks on His behalf, and the Lord expects obedience.

I have encountered members who say, "Since I am an adult, I don't need to listen to the pastor. I can make my own decisions."

> *God's obedience principle is not determined by a person's age or status in life.*

God's obedience principal is not determined by a person's age or status in life. It is based upon the fact that the Lord has appointed pastors (Ephesians 4:11) and they are the ones through which He communicates to the church.

Shepherds are commanded to feed believers with the Word of God and to look out for their spiritual welfare and progress. They are not to be forced to oversee, but must do so willingly.

Feed the flock of God which is among you, taking the oversight thereof, not by constraint, but willingly; not for filthy lucre, but of a ready mind; neither as being lords over God's heritage, but being [examples] to the flock.

1 PETER 5:2-3

WHAT'S THE MOTIVE?

Pastoral functions are not to be administered purely for remuneration. This does not mean that a minister should not be appropriately compensated, rather that they must not operate in their calling for the sole purpose of accumulating wealth.

Since pastors are to lead by example, it is imperative that their motives be spiritually based. A financial objective is not in line with God's will. Ministers of the Gospel are to focus only on winning souls, strengthening and reinforcing believers and promoting their spiritual growth.

Bringing men and women to the saving knowledge of Jesus Christ is the primary reason we engage in our call. The pastor is not to be a *Lord* of the flock, but to serve them as an overseer.

God does not set direction or give the responsibility of oversight to everyone. He achieves this – almost exclusively – through pastors.

If Satan can destroy the influence of ministers, he can impede the progress of many believers. However, when members of an assembly stand with their God-appointed spiritual leader, a wall of resistance is raised against the devil's attack.

A MATTER OF RESPECT

On more than one occasion I have been a recipient of the disrespect of believers, and I have seen other pastors receive the same treatment. In some instances, irreverence received from church members is the same as that received from the unsaved. I realize that some pastors lack the possession of a shepherd's heart and some conduct themselves in an ungodly manner, yet the vast majority of pastors are doing things God's way.

- Not *all* pastors are working schemes to achieve material prosperity.
- Not *all* pastors are involved in adulterous relationships.
- Not *all* pastors are stealing money from their local assemblies.
- Not *all* pastors have problems with addictive substances.
- Not *all* pastors mistreat their wives and families.
- Not *all* pastors are callous and cold toward believers under their watch and care.
- Not *all* pastors are too busy to interact with their church members.
- Not *all* pastors are abusers of young men and women.

- Not *all* pastors are homosexuals.
- Not *all* pastors are vindictive and unforgiving.
- Not *all* pastors are proud and arrogant.
- Not *all* pastors are selfish and unconcerned about the welfare of believers.

I pray that the point I am making is clear. In every profession there are good and bad, competent and incompetent people. Believers, therefore, should not disrespect *all* pastors simply because of their exposure to some who may have been ungodly in the performance of their calling.

The truth is, when only a *few* ministers of the Gospel fail, their stories are blasted in the news as if it is the norm, not the exception.

> *When only a few ministers of the Gospel fail, their stories are blasted in the news as if it is the norm, not the exception.*

"TOUCH NOT!"

When the Lord said, *"Touch not mine anointed, and do my prophets no harm"* (Psalm 105:15), He was speaking to the laity. In that same chapter, He referred to them as the "seed of Abraham" (v.6) – God's chosen children.

The Lord never forgot His covenant with Abraham that was confirmed with Isaac and Jacob. He promised to give them their inheritance in the land of Canaan – even when their numbers were small and there were strangers in the camp. As they journeyed from one nation and kingdom to another, the Lord covered them with His protection.

God's command to *"do my prophets no harm"* is broad in its scope. It applies to presidents and kings, as well as members of a congregation.

Every individual who calls themselves a member of the Body of Christ should seek to exemplify the biblical standard of pastoral respect. When that regard is lacking, believers then begin to "touch" Gods anointed.

Many seem to think that if they have not physically laid their hands upon their pastors, they have not *touched* them. This is not true. When words are spoken against a pastor, that individual is *verbally* touched. The minister may not be aware of what was said, yet I can assure you *God is aware*. This is why Christians must resist the urge to speak against their pastors.

> *When words are spoken against a pastor, that individual is verbally touched.*

It is inappropriate for believers to come against those God has appointed. Church members are not to overlook wrongdoing, rather seek resolution through properly established channels.

DAVID WAS CONVICTED

To better understand why the Lord expects us to respect an anointed leader, let us look at the lives of Saul and David.

For some time King Saul pursued David to kill him because Samuel – by God's direction – had anointed David to be the next king of the nation of Israel.

The book of 1 Samuel 24 describes how David had an opportunity to kill Saul, yet did not.

When King Saul walked into the cave at Engedi, David and his men remained at the sides of the entrance. David's men, however, insisted that the Lord had delivered Saul to David so he could kill him. What was David's response? He arose and simply cut of the skirt of Saul's robe. After doing so, David's heart convicted him for doing it. He said to his men:

The Lord forbid that I should do this thing unto my master, the Lord's anointed, to stretch forth mine hand against him, seeing he is the anointed of the Lord.

1 SAMUEL 24:6

Even more, David refused to allow any of his servants to harm or kill Saul. In 1 Samuel 26, David and Abishai came to the people by night and found Saul asleep. Abishai told David that the Lord had delivered Saul into his hand. He requested that David allow him to smite Saul with the spear. Once more, David said:

Destroy him not: for who can stretch forth his hand

against the Lord's anointed, and be guiltless!
1 SAMUEL 26:9

David's only actions were to remove Saul's spear and take a cruse of water before they departed. Then, standing on the top of a hill, David called to Saul's camp and revealed what he had done. There was such a respect for God's anointing that David refused to harm Saul.

DANGERS OF DISRESPECT

It is a serious matter to come against a pastor who has been chosen, called and anointed by the Lord. A spiritual covering has been placed over their lives by the presence and power of the Holy Spirit. To disrespect an anointed servant is to come against God – and against the people He has placed under that person's watch-care.

- To come against a pastor is to question God's anointing on that minister – and what the Lord intends to do through that individual to expand His kingdom.
- To come against a pastor is to disregard the call that Almighty God has placed upon him.
- To come against a pastor is to say that God should be chastising that individual, yet is not.
- To come against a pastor is to put oneself into the position of God, since it is *He* who brings reproof to His chosen representatives.

The Lord has a procedure for dealing with unruly pastors – either judging directly or through an established ecclesiastical order. He has never directed church members to become involved in such issues.

Paul stated how they are to be treated:

> ~
> *The Lord has a procedure for dealing with unruly pastors – either judging directly or through an established ecclesiastical order.*

Let the elders that rule well be counted worthy of double honour, especially they who labour in word and doctrine.

1 TIMOTHY 5:17

The elders Paul spoke of were preachers of the Word. They are to be treated with *twice* the honor – not to elevate the leaders as a god, rather to reflect the esteem a minister deserves.

There seems to be a few in every congregation who shun any opportunity to pay respect to their spiritual leader. They refuse to participate in specials days of tribute or designated gifts to the pastor. Such individuals are only robbing themselves of a blessing.

Every Bible-believing man or woman of God should show their thanks to those who *labor in word and doctrine* on their behalf. Dedicated pastors spend many hours in Bible study, fasting, prayer, sermon research and preparation.

THE ISSUE OF COMPENSATION

If a productive person is not properly cared for, production will stop. Here's how Paul made the point:

> *For the scripture saith, Thou shalt not*
> *muzzle the ox that treadeth out the corn. And,*
> *The labourer is worthy of his reward.*
>
> 1 TIMOTHY 5:18

How do you get the most work from an ox? It happens when he is appropriately fed and treated well. Likewise, pastors can better achieve what God has called them to do when they are properly cared for.

Some make the mistake of thinking ministers have a cushy job – that they float through life being overpaid for their actual duties. "After all, it's just Wednesday night and Sundays, isn't it?" Far from it!

The average minister labors far above the normal 40 hours a week. As I often say, "I officially punched in for work on November 24, 1985, when God used me to establish the Church Of The Redeemed Of The Lord, and I have never punched out."

A pastor is always on call – 24 hours a day. Even when on vacation he can expect an emergency phone call from a family in crisis or to perform a funeral.

Sermon preparation is only part of the schedule. A spiritual leader becomes a counselor, a comforter to the sick and shut-ins, a participant in countless committee meetings and the Chief Executive Officer.

Is it any wonder their families complain, "Why can't you spend more time with us?"

A BIBLICAL PRINCIPLE

Every church member needs to grasp the magnitude of a pastor's unrelenting responsibilities. They have been given an enormous responsibility and should be compensated appropriately.

Why should pastors take vows of poverty when Jesus came so we could all have abundant life – which includes both spiritual and material prosperity?

Those who believe that a minister should be poor to stay humble don't understand the biblical principle of sowing and reaping.

Those who believe that a minister should be poor to stay humble don't understand the biblical principle of sowing and reaping. If a pastor invests his total life into God's work, he should receive his just reward – not only in heaven, but on earth. If the church flourishes, so should the shepherd.

Here's what the Bible has to say on the topic:

*Be not deceived: God is not mocked: for
whatsoever a man soweth, that shall he also reap.*
GALATIANS 6:7

*But this I say, He which soweth sparingly
shall reap also sparingly: and he which soweth
bountifully shall reap also bountifully.*
2 CORINTHIANS 9:6

*And God is able to make all grace abound toward
you: that ye, always having all sufficiency in all
things, may abound to every good work.*
1 CORINTHIANS 9:8

*Give, and its shall be given unto you: good measure,
pressed down, and shaken together, and running over,
shall men give into your bosom. With the same measure
that ye mete withal it shall be measured to you again.*
LUKE 6:38

These verses make it obvious that God wants to abundantly bless *all* His people. By the very nature of their calling, minsters invest their life, labor – and even *lucre* – into the ministry to which they have been assigned.

THE BASIS OF BLESSING

I am firmly convinced that the level of success some ministers have achieved has come as a direct result of God's laws of seedtime and harvest. Certainly, there are a few men of the cloth who have wrongfully accumulated wealth. Again, they are the exceptions, not the rule.

Many who proclaim the Gospel are blessed simply because they have continually blessed others. Over the years of our ministry, I have experienced the abundance of the Lord, yet I have never worked harder in my life - both physically and emotionally.

To grow from a handful of members to more than five thousand took much fasting, praying, and untold hours of intense labor. There are some, however, who still believe the pastor should not enjoy the normal comforts of life. Somehow they conclude that their ten dollar tithe and five dollar offering are the means for the pastor's prosperity. They don't understand that *Jesus* is the reason people are blessed – whether the person is in the pulpit or the pew.

Many who proclaim the Gospel are blessed simply because they have continually blessed others.

Don't misunderstand. I'm not saying that pastors should, first and foremost, live in mansions, possess fleets of automobiles, and employ butlers and maids. I do believe, however, that if the Lord bountifully rewards a minister of the Gospel to that level, believers should recognize it as the blessing of the Lord, not the pastor's highest priority.

None of us should be jealous or annoyed when the laws of sowing and reaping are manifested in the lives of others.

"JUST LIKE ME!"

Some people try to place themselves and the minister on equal footing, saying, "He's a man, just like I am." "She's human just like me." Or, "He puts his pants on the same way I do."

It is true, we were all created equally in God's family:

So God created man in his own image, in the image of God created he him: male and female created he them.

GENESIS 2:7

And the Lord God formed a man of the dust of the ground, and breathed into his nostrils the breath of life; and man became a living soul.

GENESIS 2:4

Even though we are all in the human family, we are *positionally* different. Unbelievers are positioned in Satan, while believers are positioned in Christ. Within the church, we are given a specific place according to the purpose of God for our lives.

> *Even though we are all in the human family, we are positionally different.*

To the Christian in Corinth, the Apostle Paul explained that just as a person has many parts, so does the church. He said, *"Now ye are the body of Christ, and members in particular"* (1 Corinthians 12:27). Then he continued: *"And God has set some in the church, first apostles, secondarily prophets, thirdly teachers..."* (v.28).

This means that each of us has been called to perform certain Kingdom functions and God has planted the ability in us to accomplish them. He has equipped us so He can use us at His designated time.

With each appointment comes responsibility. He places the spiritual obligation upon us to perform His bidding in a reliable and trustworthy manner. With duty comes accountability. We have to give an account to God concerning the way we perform the assignments for which we are responsible.

The place of a pastor is a significant position in the Body of Christ. It carries a tremendous weight of responsibility – to be the overseer of God's people.

GOD'S ANGELS

In the second and third chapters of the Book of Revelation, the pastors of the seven churches of Asia Minor are referred to as *angels* – messengers of the Almighty. This is reflective of what the life quality of pastors is expected to be.

A minister who has not maintained a Godly walk will lose respect. I realize that no one is perfect but God, but there are standards of spiritual integrity that we as pastors must achieve and maintain. As ministers of the Word, our transgressions greatly impact those under our watch-care and brings reproach to the Gospel.

Scripture gives this warning:

*Woe be unto the pastors that destroy and scatter the
sheep of my pasture saith the Lord. Therefore thus saith
the Lord God of Israel against the pastors that feed my
people: Ye have scattered my flock. and driven them away.
and have not visited them: behold I will visit upon you the
evil of your doings, saith the Lord. And I will gather the
remnant of my flock out of all countries whither I have
driven them, and will bring them again to their folds; and
they shall be fruitful and increase. And I will set up shepherds over them which shall feed them: and they
shall fear no more. nor be dismayed. neither shall
they be lacking. saith the Lord.*

JEREMIAH 23:1-4

It is clear that pastors are not just simply human beings,
they are God's angels to His local churches. Their responsibilities are many and they are answerable to God. As
ministers of the Gospel, we must raise the standard of
Godliness and maintain it at increasingly higher levels. We
must conduct ourselves in a manner that exemplifies the
Lord Jesus Christ.

It is time for us (pastors) to become more than just
another man or woman. We must take our proper places in
watching over the church. We cannot lead believers to levels
of Godliness that we ourselves have not achieved. As
shepherds appointed by God, we must be examples of holy
vessels before the Father.

The Lord has ordained those in each part of His kingdom for a special purpose – both church members and

pastors. Each has a responsibility before God.

~

I have written these words to encourage Christians everywhere to take good care of those the Lord has called to look after your very soul. Pray for them, encourage them and provide whatever assistance you can to lighten the burden of their load.

1. H.B. London, Jr. and Neil B. Wiseman, Pastors at Risk, (Wheaton, Illinois: Victor Books, 1993) pp. 34,35,42,46,114,115,127,166.

~

CHAPTER FIVE

MULTIPLYING THE VISION

Thankfully, a pastor is not required to bear the entire burden alone. In almost every church setting there is a team of ministers – some on staff and others volunteer – who have been given the responsibility of helping the leader of the congregation.

These men and women are *extensions* of the pastor who are spread throughout the ministry to represent the spiritual leadership. It's impossible for the senior pastor to be everywhere and handle every situation which arises, so the ministerial staff must aid in meeting the needs of the church.

The position of the staff is uniquely different from the laity. They do not receive the vision directly from God, but indirectly through the pastors – the same as a church member. Like the pastor, however, they help in the distribution of the vision and are accountable to the minister for the role they play. (This is stated with the understanding that all of us are ultimately accountable to God).

MOSES AND THE ELDERS

The Lord has always used a team approach.

On their journey to the Promised Land, the children of Israel were supernaturally guided with a cloud by day and a fire by night. God supplied them with miraculous provisions – even manna from heaven!

Still the people complained. Many wanted to return to the fish, cucumbers melons and onions of Egypt, (Numbers 11:5).

Moses cried, "Lord, I need Your help. I can't handle all of these unhappy people by myself!"

Moses saw their discontent and cried out to God, *"I am not able to bear all this people alone, because it is too heavy for me"* (v.14).

The leader God had chosen was saying, "Lord, I need Your help. I can't handle all of these unhappy people by myself!" The burden was so great that Moses even spoke of dying (v.15).

What was God's response to His servant?

And the Lord said unto Moses, gather unto me seventy men of the elders of Israel, whom thou

knowest to be the elders of the people, and officers
over them; and bring them unto the tabernacle of the
congregation, that they may stand there with thee. And
I will come down and talk with thee there: and I will take
of the spirit which is upon thee, and will put it upon
them; and they shall bear the burden of the people
with thee, that thou bear it not thyself alone.

NUMBERS 11:16-17

God's answer included four actions – two were to be accomplished by Moses, and two by the Lord:

1. "Gather unto me seventy men of the elders of Israel."

Those chosen were to be spiritual men from the nation of Israel – not from some other background.

Likewise, staff ministers must be mature individuals who are full of the Holy Spirit:

- Their stand with God and His appointed pastor must be tried and proven.
- There must be no doubt about their commitment to God's vision through the pastor.
- They must understand the importance of following leadership and fully humble themselves to it.
- They must not obstruct God's vision with their own ministries or personal agendas.

2. *Bring them unto the tabernacle of the*
   congregation, that they may stand there with
   thee."

The elders were to stand with Moses in the sacred place. This signified that they identified with him as he led the nation under God's direction. It was an outward manifestation of their unity and bond with the man of God.

> *When the elders went to the taberncle, they were actually positioning themselves for greater responsibility from the Cord.*

When the elders went to the tabernacle, they were actually positioning themselves for greater responsibility from the Lord.

This is a model of how ministers must follow God's direction and be aligned with their pastors for the task ahead.

3. *"I will come down and talk with thee there."*

After Moses and the seventy elders were at their assigned posts, the Lord promised to descend and converse with Moses.

When we follow God's directions, He will continue His work through us. Staff ministers must be in sync with their pastor – the person who has been chosen by God to receive

His vision for the local church.

4. "I will take of the spirit which is upon thee, and I will put it upon them."

For the children of Israel to continue their journey through the wilderness, it was necessary that the leadership be in unity. That's why the Lord said He was going to take the spirit that was resting on Moses and place it upon the seventy elders.

~

For the children of Israel to continue their journey through the wilderness, it was necessary that the leadership be in unity.

Staff ministers must position themselves, and submit to, their spiritual leader, so that God can take of the spirit that dwells within the pastor and place it upon them. Together, they will work to fulfill what the Lord has prepared.

AN INGREDIENT FOR GROWTH

My experience – and that of many other ministers I have spoken with – is that many staff ministers do not realize their need for the spirit that is upon their pastors. Somehow they feel that their success in ministry will be based on other factors.

These individuals need to realize that if they do not

receive the pastor's spirit, they will miss a main ingredient of their ministerial growth and development. Also, they will not have maximum effectiveness in their work and ministry.

You may ask, "Doesn't the Lord birth a vision in the heart of staff ministers regarding what they are to do with their lives?" Of course, He does. However, as long as that person is accountable to a particular pastor, he or she must learn to fully support the vision of that individual.

> *If staff members do not receive the pastor's spirit, they will miss a main ingredient of their ministerial growth and development.*

The time will come for the staff ministers to launch out from their present situation and begin the ministry to which God has called them. Until that moment, however, their loyalty and efforts must center around what the Lord has directed the pastor to pursue.

Here are the responsibilities of staff ministers:

- To stand with the pastor in full support of the vision.
- To allow the Lord to place the spirit of the pastor upon them.
- To place what God is doing through the pastor

before their own ministry and goals.
- To aid the pastor in every way in distributing the vision to the laity.
- To always show full support of the pastor, and never speak a word against the spiritual leader or his approach to ministry, even when they seem unable to agree with it.
- To aid the pastor in training other believers to assume responsibilities in fulfilling God's plan.
- To engage in spiritual warfare in defense of God's vision fulfillment activities.

WHAT ABOUT THE LAITY?

Without the active participation of those who comprise the Body of Christ, what God is seeking to do in the local assembly will remain stagnant. For example, as a minister of the Gospel, the Lord can birth a great master-plan for our church within my soul. If, however, the members of the congregation turn a deaf ear to what the Lord is showing me, very little will be accomplished.

That is why it is important for the pastor, the staff and the laity to be in unity – working according to God's governing principles for the church.

When church members come along side of the pastor to see the work go forward, two powerful forces are unleashed:

1. The activities of the vision provide help to the laity.

2. The laity provides support for the program, in prayer and finances.

OBJECTIVES TO EMBRACE

Church members are the army of God's plan. Many are on the front line of spiritual warfare – demonstrating their determination to see the work prosper.

> *Church members are the army of God's plan.*

If a local assembly is to realize its potential, lay members should embrace these spiritual objectives:

- To humble themselves to the leading of the Holy Spirit as He reveals God's vision to them through the pastor.
- To be empowered by the Holy Spirit to receive what the Lord is revealing.
- To provide dedicated lives to advance God's program.
- To provide necessary funds for vision activities.
- To witness to others so they can also be won to the Lord and join the cause.
- To support in anyway they can, those who are involved in seeing the purpose of the church fulfilled.
- To gain a thorough understanding of God's plan through the pastor, and help bring others to the

same level of understanding.
- To defend the vision when it is opposed.
- To stand in full support of the pastor and church staff members.

There may be times when the laity doesn't understand certain actions being taken by the pastor. That's when it is necessary to continue with the vision by faith. This is more easily achieved with a spiritual leader who has proven to be faithful and committed to the Lord.

Remember, God knows exactly what He is doing, and how you and I fit perfectly into His plans.

CHAPTER SIX

~

POWERFUL, LIFE-CHANGING RESULTS

Have you ever had one of those "Wow!" moments – when it seemed like a light suddenly turned on in your brain and you said, "I've got it!"?

I believe that is how you will feel when the message of this book finally clicks in your mind, heart and soul. You'll be like Saul on the road to Damascus, when, *"suddenly there shined round about him a light from heaven"* (Acts 9:3).

Saul not only had a life-transforming conversion, the Lord even changed his name to Paul – the man who would carry the message of Christ to the known world.

The revelation God will give to you will also change everything about your life. As we will see, it affects your purpose, your marriage, your career, and much more.

1. The Vision and
Purpose Fulfillment

We serve a *purposeful* God – and whatever He does is filled with divine intent. When He made man, each person was given a specific reason for being.

Everything we need to accomplish God's will has been placed within us – He is only waiting for us to make our decision. As believers become involved in the vision God has given to the local church, here is how they will grow and develop:

- They will discover God's purpose for their lives.
- They will receive proper instruction from their pastors concerning aligning their lives with God's will.
- They will learn to walk in their calling.
- They will discover and learn to properly utilize their gifts and abilities.
- They will understand the importance of their reason for being as they interact with other believers.
- They will learn to be humble before God and those He has placed over them.
- They will gain a greater appreciation of the sacrificial death of Jesus Christ as they experience His work in their lives.
- They will learn to engage in spiritual warfare in

defense of God's Kingdom and agenda.

- They will mature in their Bible study, prayer lives, and fasting.
- They will increase their knowledge of the ways of God.
- They will discover the vital role their pastors play in God's vision, and will learn to support them.
- They will understand that God's purpose for their lives is fulfilled by adopting what the Lord has revealed through their spiritual leadership.

It is through our active involvement in God's vision that we discover and develop our purpose, and deliver to God, that which He originally intended.

2. THE VISION AND
GENERATIONAL CURSES

*Therefore if any man be in Christ, he is a
new creature: old things are passed away;
behold, all things are become new.*
2 CORINTHIANS 5:17

The born again experience positions us in Christ and breaks the curse of sin. Yet, there are often deeply rooted habits and patterns that still remain in some lives.

In addition, there may be acquired or *generational* influences which have yet to be removed. These can include: *marital infidelity, alcoholism, criminal behavior, psychological disorders, spousal abuse, child abuse and molestation, welfare mentalities, drug addiction, gambling, thievery, divorce, godlessness, academic failure and economic depravity.*

I am thankful Jesus came to free us from every bondage.

Christ hath redeemed us from the curse of the law, being made a curse for us: for it is written. Cursed is every one that hangeth on a tree: That the blessing of Abraham might come on the Gentiles through Jesus Christ: that we might receive the promise of the Spirit through faith.

GALATIANS 3:13-14

I have seen generational curses and other habits miraculously disappear when an individual embraces God's vision. These are some of the benefits:

- Our harmony with God's vision brings deliverance from generational curses and influences.
- We become one with Christ and separate from the things of the world.
- God's intention for our lives will be protected and fulfilled by Him through us.
- God will deliver us of generational curses because the negative influence will not only impact us, but others.

Some may say, "I am doing everything I can, yet I still have not been delivered."

My response is to stay with the vision and wait patiently upon the Lord. He will, according to His Word, remove every curse. God created you to perform an important role in His total plan, and He will not allow you to remain in debt to Satan – nor will He permit you to be destroyed. You can declare with

> *God created you to perform an important role in His total plan.*

full confidence, "Goodbye Satan and your evil influences. I'm working with God. You are history!"

3. THE VISION AND
THE MARRIAGE RELATIONSHIP

*Therefore shall a man leave his father and his mother,
and shall cleave unto his wife: and they shall be one flesh.*
GENESIS 2:24

The beauty in the marriage relationship, as established by God, lies in the fact that the husband and wife become one. As they live for the Lord and grow together, they are joined in the Holy Spirit, and in their own spirits.

Unfortunately, far too many couples never achieve or

experience the beauty of marital oneness. As a result, troubled and broken marriages adversely affect the church. If the families are strong, then the church will be strong – if they are weak, the church will be weak.

Here is what happens when a husband and wife live according to God's purpose. What they learn about the vision also applies to their marriage.

- They learn to express love.
- They learn fellowship and harmony.
- They learn trust.
- They learn commitment.
- They learn sacrifice.
- They learn submission.
- They learn suffering.
- They learn unity.

A major benefit of adhering to God's plan is spiritual maturity. Those who are involved in its fulfillment find themselves in a continual state of growth and development – a solidifying factor in any marital relationship.

4. THE VISION AND
CAREER FULFILLMENT

A significant number of believers today are busily engaged in secular careers. Many have acquired college and university degrees and possess great knowledge and talent –

from administration to construction, from music to teaching skills.

I am a firm believer in tithing, giving a portion of our substance back to God. Yet, have you ever wondered how far the work of the Lord would progress if each member also tithed their *abilities?* There would be an explosion of growth in the church!

If the Lord has blessed us to excel in our professions, we should be willing to give back to Him. As I shared with our congregation, "I wouldn't want this church to be deficient in any area where I have expertise."

~

Have you ever wondered how far the work of the Lord would progress if each member also tithed their abilities?

In every fellowship there is a vast pool of resources. As our church has progressed, many of our people have caught the vision and are making significant contributions of their abilities. Our current multi-million dollar facility could not have been completed without the "sweat equity" of those in our congregation who gave of their time and talent. Simply stated, their skills were used to promote God's vision.

What happens when believers fail to use their skills to advance God's Kingdom? The local church is forced to spend its budget to pay for those same services. Of course, people should be compensated where appropriate – and the church should never take advantage of a member's willingness to help.

What I am concerned about is the heart of the believer. Do they understand the blessing they will receive by offering their best to the Master? Remember, the Lord placed gifts and abilities within us that we are to use for His glory.

When we exercise our talents – keeping God at the center – He will prosper us, even advancing our careers.

But seek ye first the kingdom of God,
and his righteousness: and all these
things shall be added unto you.

MATTHEW 6:33

5. THE VISION AND
GIFT PERFECTION

For to one is given by the Spirit the word of wisdom;
to another the word of knowledge by the same Spirit;
To another faith by the same Spirit; to another the gifts
of healing by the same Spirit; To another the working
of miracles; to another prophecy; to another divers kinds
of tongues; to another the interpretation of tongues.

1 CORINTHIANS 12:8-10

The topic of spiritual gifts divides many in the Body of Christ. Nevertheless, these have been placed in the church by the Lord to foster the fulfillment of His vision.

By God's grace, I have personally experienced a number of these gifts and have seen them in operation in the lives of other believers. Unfortunately, I have also seen them abused by some Christians who view the gifts as a means of receiving recognition, popularity, and even finances.

I have never known a period in church history such as the present – when so many are claiming to be prophets and prophetesses. I must confess, however, that seldom have I encountered such a person who operates with accuracy and detail.

If you want to see prophets who were precise, read Daniel 7,8,9 as he looked past the church age and saw the events of the Book of Revelation. Observe how Isaiah spoke of the coming of Christ(Isaiah 7:14;9:6;11:1-2).

I can't begin to keep track of the prophecies which have been directed toward me that did not come true. Dates and times for events to occur in my life have come and gone, and, in almost every case, were inaccurate. I can only conclude that many who claim to possess spiritual gifts *do not* – and they are harming the cause of Christ.

Failed prophecies promote doubt and skepticism among believers and non-believers alike. Supposed healings achieve the same negative result.

Despite all the controversy surrounding spiritual gifts, they are still evident and powerfully used by the Lord. There *are* individuals in the Body of Christ who operate in the gifts with accuracy. When this happens the church is gloriously advanced.

Identification with God's vision will bring the most powerful and effective operation in the gifts of the Spirit. They are used in many ways:

- They manifest the miraculous power of God.
- They are instrumental in spiritual warfare against the enemy.
- They give insight into the lives of believers, thereby providing the basis for helping them.
- They offer the ability to effect change for the continuity of the advancement of God's vision.
- They are an effective witness in the winning of souls.
- They are a major source of strength and encouragement.

As we promote God's purpose, He will assure the perfection of the gifts He has placed in us so they can be effectively used to advance His vision.

6. The Vision and
The Anointing

When God called us, He had Kingdom assignments waiting – and, through His Holy Spirit, He anoints us to accomplish them. The anointing removes burdens and destroys the devastating yokes of bondage.

To achieve our purpose, the Lord has empowered us to fulfill specific functions. For example, there is the *psalmist anointing* to tear down resistant barriers to praise and worship. There is the *administrative anointing* to empower believers to effectively carry on the organizational duties within the Body of Christ. There is the *anointing to teach and preach* the Word of God.

The Old Testament includes this story. After God rejected Saul, He commanded Samuel to anoint one of Jesse's sons to be the next king. At Jesse's house, Samuel saw Jesse's son Eliab and thought he was the one to be anointed, but God rejected him and told Samuel that *"man looks at the outward appearance, but the Lord looketh on the heart"* (1 Samuel 16:7).

Jesse asked that seven of his sons pass before Samuel, but none was approved by God to be anointed. Samuel inquired "Do you have any more sons?" They sent for David, and when he arrived, the Lord told Samuel to anoint him in the midst of his brethren, and the *"Spirit of the Lord"* came upon him (v.13).

God had a vision for the nation of Israel and David was anointed to play a major role in completing it.

Today, Jesus Christ is the "Anointed One," and the anointing flows from Him to those of us who comprise His Body. It is needed to overthrow demonic powers, to remove enemy strongholds, to carry on kingdom business in the face of enemy opposition and to divinely enable believers in the progression of God's vision.

Every Christian is of importance and each has attributes

the Lord wants to anoint. He pours His Spirit on the voices of believers He calls to sing, and to those He calls to preach the Gospel, or to be counselors or missionaries.

Once we are touched by God, we will never be the same. When Saul was spiritually empowered to become the first king of Israel, the Bible says that he was *"turned into another man"* (1 Samuel 10:6).

> *Our anointing will be no greater than our personal dedication and commitment to the advancement of God's vision.*

Our anointing will be no greater than our personal dedication and commitment to the advancement of God's vision. Those who are out of step will never achieve what is possible in their lives.

On numerous occasions I have seen men and women deliver the Word in an impressive manner, yet few lives were spiritually touched. What was missing? The power that comes with the anointing.

Those who resist the vision leadership of their shepherd will soon realize that their engagement in the Lord's work is without His approval. If a believer cannot follow God's chosen leadership, neither can that person be trusted with God's anointing.

The choice is yours. If you want to receive everything the Lord has to offer, pursue His vision.

7. THE VISION AND
THE UNITY OF THE
BODY OF CHRIST

*Behold, how good and how pleasant it
is for brethren to dwell together in unity.*

PSALM 133:1

When God formed the church, He eliminated the gulf between Jews and Gentiles. There were some lingering attitudes, but the church provided the means by which all could come together. In Christ, distinctions were abolished – there would be no "Jewish Church of Christ" or "Gentile Church Of Christ."

To be in unity with the Lord we must partner ourselves with Him – to think like Him, to live like Him.

This *oneness* must also be expressed in the church. As Paul wrote, *"For as the body is one, and hath many members, and all the members of that one body, being many, are one body, so also is Christ"* (1 Corinthians 12:2).

In order for harmony to exist, each church member must perform the functions for which they are equipped. They must also empathize with the suffering of other Christians, and rejoice when others rejoice.

When each believer adheres to the vision, a bond of unity will result:

■ It causes all of us to work toward a common goal.

- It provides a vision fulfillment plan for us to follow and a clear delineation of Kingdom activities.
- It produces the maximum use of our gifts and callings.
- It manifests the importance of each believer in God's overall plan, while gaining an understanding of the role of others.
- It creates a proper atmosphere for the exchange of vital Kingdom knowledge.
- It promotes the helping and assisting of one another in meeting Kingdom and personal needs.
- It provides a collective body of individuals who possess needed resources.
- It guarantees quality leaders and followers because everyone is adhering to the vision.
- It prevents the intrusion of division.
- It is an established standard for spiritual work and conduct.
- It is a manifestation of the fact that the gates of hell shall not prevail against the Church.

~

God's vision is much more than a wishful dream to be desired. It is the driving force of the church and, when we embrace it, brings powerful, life-changing results.

~

CHAPTER SEVEN

IT'S YOUR DECISION

I sincerely believe that every child of God must be actively involved in progressing God's vision. We have been saved and equipped by the Lord for a reason – so that we can be used by Him to advance the Kingdom.

No longer can we afford to sit back and allow a remnant group of believers to overwork themselves performing what the Lord expects of *every* church member.

To put it in common language, "It's time to fish or cut bait!"

Those who call themselves Christians need to take a bold step forward and say, "Pastor, here are my gifts and abilities. How can I help to see God's work prosper?"

HEAVEN'S ASSIGNMENT

The Lord must be given the *highest* priority in our lives,

not only when we are first saved, but months, years and decades later. This requires dedication, sacrifice and endurance.

Bringing the Father's desire into reality is a joint effort – an assignment given to the *entire* Body of Christ. It was never God's intention that a few believers be overworked and overwhelmed by the task, while the majority sit back and enjoy the benefits.

> ⌒
>
> *Bringing the Father's desire into reality is a joint effort – an assignment given to the entire Body of Christ.*

As the church advances, those who are actively involved will be abundantly blessed. Just as important, many who are outside the ark of safety will be saved.

What a wonderful testimony to the world when they see a congregation that is totally unified! Sadly, when the unsaved look at the church today, they often see strife and division. It's the wrong message!

For the sake of Christ, it is time to set aside our differences and become what God intends for us to be. As a result, the Body of Christ will be blessed collectively, and believers will be blessed individually.

Let the nations see what the Lord envisions for His church.

TIME TO DECIDE

On these pages you have learned that God has a divine blueprint – an orderly plan – to bring His vision into reality. It involves me – it involves you.

- Are you ready to see God's purpose realized through your life?
- Will you submit to spiritual leadership according to God's divine order?
- Will you present your gifts and talents to see the church move forward?
- Are you ready to receive God's anointing for service?
- Will you put the Father's love into daily practice?
- Are you ready to commit your relationships to Him?
- Will you allow the Lord to perfect His gifts in your life?
- Are you prepared to do your part in bringing unity to the Body of Christ?
- Will you make a total commitment to God's vision?

It is your decision!

FOR A COMPLETE LIST OF BOOKS
AND TAPES BY DR. JEROME STOKES,
CONTACT:

CHURCH OF THE REDEEMED OF THE LORD
4321 OLD YORK ROAD
BALTIMORE, MD 21212

PHONE 1-866-THE LAMP (843-5267)

QUANTITY DISCOUNTS OF
GOD'S VISION, YOUR DECISION
BY JEROME STOKES

Place the message of this important book into the hands of your entire church family.
- Present a copy to each member of your congregation.
- Give a copy to each person upon becoming a member of your church.

Individual books may be ordered through any book store. Quantity discounts of up to 50% are available direct from the publisher. The books are shipped in case lots of 50 books per case. Photocopy or clip the following order form.

DISCOUNT ORDER FORM: GOD'S VISION, YOUR DECISION

Cases	# of Books	Discount	Your cost per $12.95 book	Total	Your Order
1	50	30%	$ 9.07	$453.25	$
2	100	40%	7.77	777.00	$
3	150	50%	6.48	971.25	$
___	___	50%	6.48	$____	$

Add shipping and handling of $9 per case: $_____

Total check or money order enclosed: $_____

Ship to:

Name: _____

Organization: _____

Address: _____

City/State/Zip:_____

Phone #: _____

Send this discount order form (and make check payable) to:
LIFEBRIDGE BOOKS
P.O. BOX 49428
CHARLOTTE, NC 28277